MW01131478

Focusing on Fitness

Have You Got What It Takes to Be a Personal Trainer?

by Lisa Thompson

Compass Point Books ✦ Minneapolis, Minnesota

First American edition published in 2008 by
Compass Point Books
3109 West 50th Street, #115
Minneapolis, MN 55410

Editor: Julie Gassman
Designer: Lori Bye
Creative Director: Keith Griffin
Editorial Director: Nick Healy
Managing Editor: Catherine Neitge
Content Adviser: Matthew J. Zens, Doctor of Physical Therapy,
        Certified Athletic Trainer, Orthopedic Institute, Sioux Falls, S.D.

Editor's note: To best explain careers to readers, the author has
created composite characters based on extensive interviews and research.

 This book was manufactured with paper containing
at least 10 percent post-consumer waste.
Printed in the United States of America

Library of Congress Cataloging-in-Publication Data
Thompson, Lisa, 1969–
Focusing on fitness : have you got what it takes to be
a personal trainer? / by Lisa Thompson.
 p. cm. — (On the job)
 Includes index.
 ISBN 978-0-7565-3619-0 (library binding)
1. Physical education and training—Vocational guidance.
2. Personal trainers—Vocational guidance. I. Title. II. Series.
 GV481.4.T46 2008
 613.7'1—dc22   2007035555

Image Credits: Shutterstock/Mikael Damkier, cover (left); Shutterstock/iofoto, cover
(right). All other images are from one of the following royalty-free sources: Big Stock
Photo, Dreamstime, Istock, Photo Objects, Photos.com, and Shutterstock. Every effort
has been made to contact copyright holders of any material reproduced in this book. Any
omission will be rectified in subsequent printings if notice is given to the publishers.

Visit Compass Point Books on the Internet at *www.compasspointbooks.com*
or e-mail your request to *custserv@compasspointbooks.com*

Table of Contents

That Winning Feeling   4
What Does a Personal Trainer Do?   8
Timetable of a Typical Day   10
How I Became a Personal Trainer   12
Other Career Options   16
Understanding the Body   18
Built for Sports   22
Basic Fitness Tests   24
Different Types of Exercise   26
Sports Nutrition   30
Training a Winning Mind   34
Personal Training and Coaching Tips   36
Shaun's Training Countdown Begins   38
Steps to Become a Personal Trainer   44
Find Out More   46
Glossary   47
Index   48

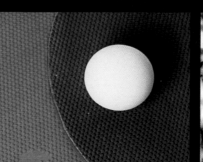

That Winning Feeling

My name is Evan, and I am a personal trainer. Right now, I'm watching Shaun, one of my clients, play basketball. It's a close game, and Shaun's team is only a few points behind. Suddenly, Shaun steals the ball. I quickly glance up at the clock. There are only seconds remaining in the game. If Shaun keeps his cool, his team has a chance of winning.

Shaun races down the side, dribbling the ball with confidence. He looks relaxed and focused. I can tell he's in the zone. He leaps up and takes the shot. It's his only chance. He scores! It's a three-pointer, and the crowd goes wild! The final buzzer sounds. It's all over.

Shaun's team has won! They are ecstatic. This win means they have a chance of winning the state championship.

As Shaun's personal trainer, I am already thinking about the game and the recovery and training that's ahead of us. The win is all the more exciting because I've been training Shaun since he recovered from a serious leg injury. Some experts thought he would never play again.

As a sports trainer, I guide athletes and people interested in improving their fitness.

PUN FUN **Those who play team sports usually have a ball.**

After the game, I listen to the coach as he explains the training schedule for the next few weeks. When everybody has settled down and absorbed the win, I talk to Shaun and discuss our training plans for the days ahead. I want 100 percent focus and commitment. I want to keep Shaun motivated and positive. He has worked hard to get where he is today. Now it is time to reap the rewards.

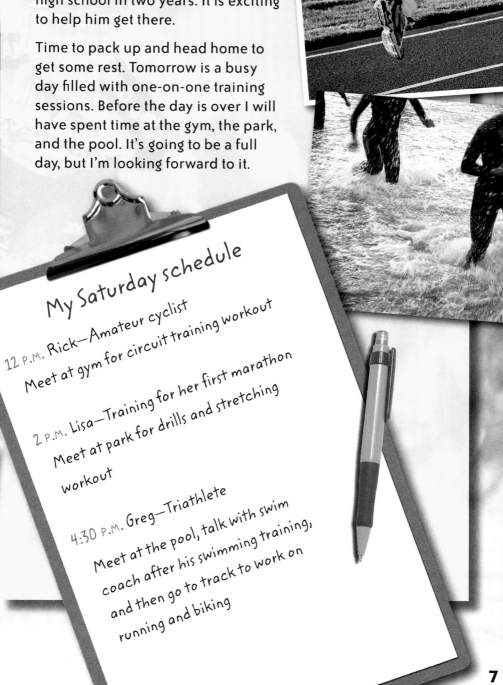

I know Shaun has what it takes to fulfill his dream of playing college basketball after he graduates from high school in two years. It is exciting to help him get there.

Time to pack up and head home to get some rest. Tomorrow is a busy day filled with one-on-one training sessions. Before the day is over I will have spent time at the gym, the park, and the pool. It's going to be a full day, but I'm looking forward to it.

My Saturday schedule

12 P.M. Rick—Amateur cyclist
Meet at gym for circuit training workout

2 P.M. Lisa—Training for her first marathon
Meet at park for drills and stretching workout

4:30 P.M. Greg—Triathlete
Meet at the pool, talk with swim coach after his swimming training, and then go to track to work on running and biking

What Does a Personal Trainer Do?

I help athletes and ordinary people achieve their fitness goals and increase their skills. I also help them decrease the risk of injuries or manage them through exercise and recovery. It's my job to help athletes perform at their best. I make sure they're in good shape and ready to play.

Stretching before working out helps prevent injury.

I teach my clients how to exercise in a way that helps prevent injuries. For example, I lead teams and individuals through stretching exercises prior to each event, during practice, and at the end of each event.

I also monitor small injuries and work out the best ways to deal with them and the recovery. If an athlete is injured, I work with doctors and physical therapists to set up a therapy routine for the athlete's recovery program.

Personal trainers need to understand what's best for their clients. They don't just push their clients hard. They encourage them to work out at levels that will help them achieve their goals. Many people need only one session to get on the right track, while others need more guidance. Some are only motivated to work hard under the watchful eye of a personal trainer.

Personal trainers need to keep up with new developments in sports science so they can best advise their clients. For example, research recommends that joggers train on grass rather than concrete. Grass is easier on the body's joints and is less likely to cause injury.

Personal trainers work in a variety of settings with individuals and teams. Trainers may work in sports clubs, gyms, health clubs, schools, universities, and spas. The work environment can be as individual as the trainers themselves.

Timetable of a Typical Day

6:30–8 A.M. Meet Rick at the gym. He is a cyclist. I am doing a weights program with him to increase his strength. We also work on his mental focus and proper technique on the stationary bike.

9 A.M. Talk to a Pilates instructor about a client who wants to increase her core strength and flexibility without weights. Together we devise a program. Part of the challenge of being a physical trainer is constantly finding and trying out new ways for clients to achieve their fitness goals.

10 A.M. Meet Lisa, who's training for a marathon. We train for 90 minutes on the beach, doing sand running.

1:30–4 P.M Answer e-mails at the office, update training and recovery programs, and monitor training and fitness results that have come in. Part of being a trainer is assessing both your own progress and the results of your clients. I organize some notes for a talk I am giving to a school about the importance of fitness and proper training in sports.

5 P.M. Meet Shaun at the basketball courts to do some drills. We then do some stretching and speed work.

6–7 P.M. Meet with a new client whose goal is to prepare for the ski season. The hour-long session includes interval and light strength training. Special emphasis is placed on balance training with trek poles that act like ski poles. I show the client how to use the stability ball for abdominal exercises and stretching. We go through the fitness plan I've drawn up for him and arrange to meet again in a week.

How I Became a Personal Trainer

I've been interested in sports since elementary school, where I was involved in swimming, basketball, and football. I competed for my school, but mostly I was into sports for fun.

As a teenager, I took up triathlons—a combination of swimming, cycling, and running. While I was never an Olympic champion, I always went out and gave it my best.

Running is lots of fun and is a very effective way of keeping fit.

After I finished high school, I went to college and studied physical education. As part of the program, I studied sports science and took many courses relating to coaching and personal training.

While in college, I was still competing in triathlons. I began to create my own training programs as a way to try out some of the things I was learning. It was also a way of improving my performance. In fact, I improved so much in one season, other athletes on campus began asking me to write their programs. Eventually I was offered a job training the university rowing team.

When I finished college, I had enough clients to become a full-time personal trainer. Most of my clients are competitive athletes, where every second or inch of improvement counts. However, I also train ordinary people who are interested in improving or maintaining their fitness.

As a personal trainer, my main goal is to nurture the skills that make a winning athlete or team, including talent, technique, and winning attitude.

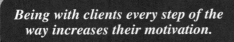

Being with clients every step of the way increases their motivation.

Personal trainer studies

Personal trainers must be familiar with a number of related areas, including sports nutrition, drugs in sports, principles of injury management, common sports injuries, sports taping, medical conditions affecting athletes, and many types of exercises. Here is a closer look at the school subjects involved.

Biology: Scientific study of living organisms

Chemistry: The study of matter and its interactions

Exercise physiology: The study of how the body works and responds to physical activity

First aid: Emergency care given to an injured person before medical aid can be obtained

Food science: Studying all aspects of food, from harvesting to consumption; includes nutrition and diet

Human anatomy: Understanding the structure and makeup of the body

Kinesiology: The scientific study of human movement

Physiology: Understanding how living organisms function

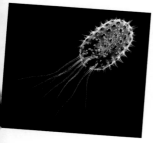

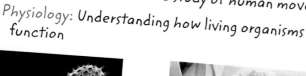

Things to keep in mind if you want to be a personal trainer

- Have a love of sports
- Be positive and motivated
- Be disciplined
- Be patient and understanding
- Be a good communicator
- Have the ability and perseverance to search for solutions
- Be ethical—do the right thing for your client

Be prepared to work long and irregular hours.

You can get a head start on your personal trainer career. Take related classes in school.

Here are a few you should be sure to include:

- biology
- physical education
- human anatomy
- chemistry

Other Career Options

There are other careers related to personal training that you may find interesting.

Sports physician

Sports physicians are doctors who specialize in sports medicine. They diagnose sports-related injuries and develop rehabilitation and recovery training programs for athletes.

Exercise physiologist

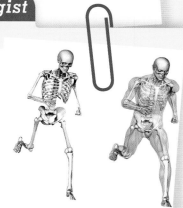

Exercise physiologists study the way the human body moves. They design and manage programs to help people recover from injury or manage pain.

Manager

Sports managers oversee the careers of athletes. They negotiate contracts and business details. They may also manage their clients' schedules.

Dietician

Dieticians understand and research the science of food (vitamins, minerals, food groups, etc.) to help people select the right food combinations to gain, maintain, and promote health.

Sports journalist

Sports journalists work for the media. They write or broadcast stories about games, events, and athletes. Sports journalists go to many events to cover stories and often work on tight deadlines.

Coach

Coaches train athletes or sports teams in order to maximize the chance of victory. They can work with athletes or teams for long-term or short-term periods.

Sports officials

Umpires, referees, judges, and other sports officials observe the play and enforce the rules of the sport. They also impose penalties if the rules are broken. These officials are often required to make decisions in a split second.

Understanding the Body

Understanding the human body enables personal trainers to develop training programs and identify, evaluate, and treat sports injuries. An understanding of the skeletal system, joints and ligaments, muscles and their attachments, and the cardio-respiratory system (the heart and lungs) is essential.

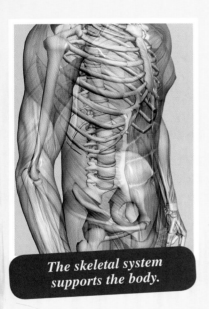

The skeletal system supports the body.

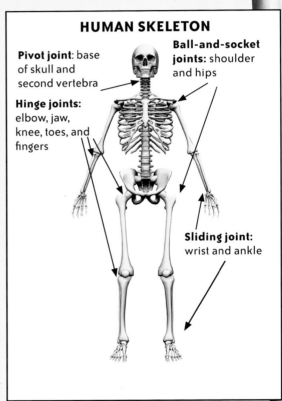

HUMAN SKELETON

Pivot joint: base of skull and second vertebra

Ball-and-socket joints: shoulder and hips

Hinge joints: elbow, jaw, knee, toes, and fingers

Sliding joint: wrist and ankle

The skeletal system

There are 206 bones in the human body. Many of them are connected by a variety of joints, allowing movement in multiple directions.

For an athlete, it is important that these joints are protected correctly to prevent injury and minimize wear and tear.

Muscle groups

One of the ways athletes can protect their joints and bones is by building and toning muscles.

Evolution has taught the body to carry just enough muscle to comfortably perform daily routines. This makes it very difficult to increase muscle mass. Also, any gained muscle is easy to lose once exercise is stopped for any length of time. To increase and maintain their muscle mass, athletes need to work out with weights regularly.

Skeletal muscles usually work in pairs, so a trainer must know a muscle's opposing muscle when developing a program. Working opposing muscles helps achieve maximum muscle balance, strength, and stability.

If one muscle is overworked at the expense of another, it may leave an athlete vulnerable to injury. Training opposite muscle groups is also one way a trainer helps an athlete recover from injury.

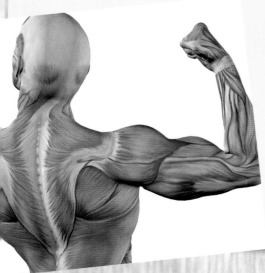

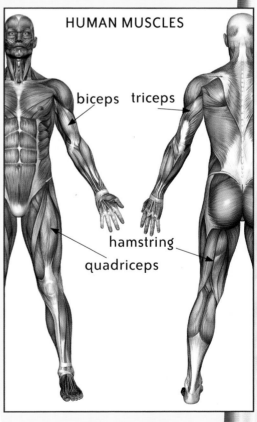

HUMAN MUSCLES

biceps   triceps

hamstring

quadriceps

The twitch advantage

Muscles are made up of fast- and slow-twitch fibers. Everyone has the same number of fibers in each muscle, although the proportion of fast to slow twitch varies from person to person.

Fast-twitch fibers contract very quickly and yield a short burst of energy. They are used whenever a sudden burst of speed or strength is needed, such as in sprinting. Slow-twitch fibers are used more in endurance sports, such as distance running.

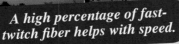
A high percentage of fast-twitch fiber helps with speed.

PUN FUN **The jogger who overslept found himself running late.**

Scientists believe that successful sprinter muscles are 70 percent fast-twitch fiber. This compares with 50 percent for the average person. This characteristic enables sprinters to explode out of the starting blocks with more speed and power.

Fascinating facts about muscles

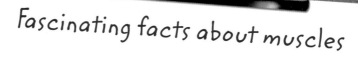

- There are approximately 650 skeletal muscles in the human body.
- About 40 percent of your weight is muscle.
- Your muscles are 75 percent water and 20 percent protein. The rest is stuff like salts, minerals, and carbohydrates.

- For their size-to-strength ratio, the muscles that operate the wings of bees, flies, and mosquitoes are stronger than any human muscles.

- One of the smallest muscles in the human body has one of the longest names. The *levator labii superioris alaeque nasi* is the tiny muscle beside your nose that raises your lip into a sneer.

Built for Sports

Human beings can be grouped into three basic body types: round, muscular, and lean and long. Everyone is a mixture of all three in different proportions. Certain sports favor particular body shapes—tall basketball players, hefty rugby players, slight gymnasts. Your body shape may make you more suited to a particular sport. Your combination may also affect the amount of muscle mass you can build, and the type of fitness program you need to stay in shape.

It helps to be stocky for games such as rugby.

It's a definite advantage for female gymnasts to be lean.

Being tall is useful for basketball players.

The body type chart

Endomorphs

Round in appearance and tend to gain weight in the abdomen area; can easily be overweight

Mesomorphs

Muscular in appearance, with wide shoulders and narrow waists; tend to build and develop muscle easily

Ectomorphs

Lean in appearance, with long legs and arms; have low fat storages so tend to be slim

Figuring out an athlete's body type formula

Sports scientists use specialized equipment to scientifically measure athletes for height, weight, length, width, circumference, and body fat.

Specialized measuring equipment

The athletes are then assigned a rating from 1 to 7 for the amount of each component in their body mix. One is the lowest, and 7 is the highest.

Athletes are then given a three-digit number. For example, 6-4-2 means that the athlete's endomorph rating is 6, the mesomorph is 4, and the ectomorph is 2.

Basic Fitness Tests

Before developing programs, I give clients some basic tests to assess their fitness levels.

A fitness assessment lets me know their baseline fitness. It also gives us something to compare to, so we can monitor progress. This allows us to see which areas need to be worked on more and those showing the most improvement.

The heart

The heart is the body's strongest muscle. It pumps blood through the body. Every beat is recorded as a pulse.

The heart supplies more blood to an exercising muscle. The harder an athlete works, the higher the pulse rate. A trainer can use an athlete's resting heart rate and maximum heart rate to see whether they're working hard enough, or too hard, and plan a program accordingly.

Circulatory system

Health forms provide general health backgrounds.

24

Measuring heart rate

Resting heart rate

The best time to take a resting heart rate is first thing in the morning, before you even get out of bed. The two most common places for measuring heart rate are the wrist and the neck.

- Using two fingers, find a pulse and count the number of beats for 10 seconds. Multiply the number of beats by six.
- This gives the heart beats per minute.
- Record the heart beat before exercise (resting heart rate) and then right after your workout (maximum heart rate).

Measuring maximum heart rate

- Find a stable step or bench.
- Begin stepping up on the step one leg at a time, using the opposite leg to come down on.
- After five minutes, record the heart rate.

Do not use your thumb to take a pulse. It has a pulse of its own that you may feel.

The safe maximum heart rate after exercise is 220 beats per minute minus your age. This gives an indication of how hard you've been working and how fit you are. The lower your heart rate, the fitter you are.

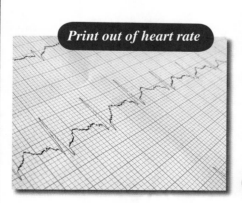
Print out of heart rate

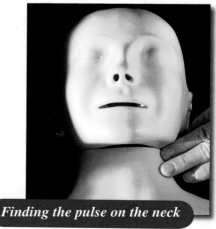
Finding the pulse on the neck

Different Types of Exercise

Personal trainers need to have a thorough knowledge of different types of sports and exercise. Both sports and exercise can be broken down into two types: aerobic and anaerobic.

Muscles need fuel in order to work. In activities such as walking, jogging, or skipping, the fuel converts to energy in the presence of oxygen. This is aerobic exercise—with air or oxygen.

When a person does strenuous work such as lifting heavy weights or sprinting, the muscles are working so intensely that not enough oxygen can get to the working muscles. Fuel must be supplied and converted to energy in a different way—anaerobically, or without air. This type of work or exercise can be done for only a short period of time before the working muscles become fatigued and must rest or slow down.

PUN FUN   **Using deodorant is no sweat.**

Aerobic

Aerobic activities can be continued for long periods of time. The heart rate increases during aerobic exercise. The heart and lungs work together to supply oxygen to the body's tissues. Aerobic exercise strengthens the heart and lungs by forcing them to work harder. It immediately increases the body's metabolic rate, or the amount of energy used, to between five and 20 times its normal rate.

Aerobic activities include cycling, rowing, or cross-country skiing. In these activities, you are using the larger muscles of the body in a rhythmical, repeated movement to get the heart rate up to "training" heart rate. A typical session lasts from 20 to 60 minutes.

Aerobic exercise makes the heart more efficient, thus lowering the risk of heart attack. It also places stress on the bones, which helps increase bone strength. It increases endurance by one-third or more, and enhances blood flow to the limbs and organs. Done regularly, aerobic activity is very good for you.

Anaerobic

During anaerobic activities, such as weight-lifting, wrestling or all-out sprinting, the working muscles are moving very fast. Because of this intensity, the movement cannot be performed for more than short periods of time—one to two minutes.

Athletes in nonendurance sports most often use anaerobic training to build power. Bodybuilders use this type of training to build muscle mass. Muscles trained under anaerobic conditions develop differently. They are able to perform better in short-duration, high-intensity activities.

Regular exercisers also benefit from anaerobic training. When you train at high levels of intensity, you increase your anaerobic threshold. This means you can work harder for longer periods of time, all while burning more calories.

Putting it all together

Most sports are a combination of aerobic and anaerobic exercise. In basketball, for example, a player running back and forth across the court operates aerobically, with occasional bursts of anaerobic energy for every jump shot or quick drive to the basket. Both aerobic and anaerobic exercises are necessary to be physically fit. Personal trainers help each client plan a balanced program with activities that are accessible, enjoyable, appropriate, and measurable.

Typical training goals

To develop a training program, understanding the base fitness of the person is just one part of it. Personal trainers must also know the athlete's training goals.

Fitness goals can be broken down into four key areas:
- **Body composition:** Clients often have the goal of increasing muscle mass and decreasing fat.
- **Flexibility:** Increased flexibility results in less pain during everyday actions. This is especially important for older clients or those suffering back pain.
- **Endurance:** Clients, especially those who compete, want to maintain their physical activity for longer periods of time.
- **Strength:** Stronger muscles help maintain weight, improve heart health, and protect joints.

PUN FUN

Seven days without exercise makes one weak.

Sports Nutrition

Food is fuel. To compete at your best, you must eat a healthy, balanced diet. I try to inspire all my clients to eat properly before and after events. I remind them that regardless of how much they train, or how dedicated they are, they will not perform at their best unless they give their bodies essential nutrients. Three types of food provide energy: carbohydrates, protein, and fat.

Carbohydrates are fuel for the body.

Carbohydrates

Carbohydrates are everyone's major fuel source. Sports dieticians recommend that complex carbohydrates such as breads, cereals, fruits, vegetables, and legumes (peas, beans, lentils) make up more than half our energy intake.

Carbohydrates are stored as glycogen in the muscles and liver. Muscles use glycogen as the main source of energy during exercise. When glycogen stores are used up, exhaustion sets in.

Protein

Protein is essential for the growth and repair of all body tissues. Athletes have slightly higher protein needs because of wear and tear on their bodies. High-protein foods include beef, tuna, chicken, oats, and cottage cheese.

Proteins work with the immune system to protect against disease.

Fat

Fat has more than twice the energy value of carbohydrates or protein. A small amount of fat is important in aiding the absorption and transportation of certain vitamins around the body. We all need dietary fat daily. A tablespoon is usually enough. Good fats tend to be liquid at room temperature (such as olive oil), while unhealthy fats are usually solid at room temperature (such as lard).

About iron

Iron is an important mineral for transporting oxygen around the body. Iron deficiency causes fatigue, because it reduces the amount of oxygen reaching the muscles. Athletes must be sure to get enough iron in order to maintain performance. Oysters, red meat, spinach, and molasses are examples of iron-rich foods.

Eating healthy fats such as olive oil helps the body absorb nutrients.

| Grains | Vegetables | Fruits | Oil | Milk | Meats/ Beans |

Glycemic index

Personal trainers can recommend foods that will maintain optimum energy levels during and after workouts. In order to do so, trainers need to know the glycemic index (GI) of foods. The GI is a ranking that measures the effect of food on blood-sugar levels over a two-hour period after the food is eaten.

A glucometer is used to measure blood-sugar levels.

Very high glucose (sugar) levels after meals are bad for general health because they damage the arteries and various blood vessels. They also promote high insulin levels, which can lead to chronic illnesses, such as diabetes. This condition, in which blood-sugar levels are above normal, can damage blood vessels and nerves. Avoiding high glucose levels is possible by eating low-GI foods. These foods supply a much steadier stream of energy. This reduces the risk of heart disease and diabetes.

Diabetics inject insulin to bring their blood-sugar levels within a normal range.

Low-GI foods

Eat before sporting event:

- baked beans
- whole wheat bread
- pasta
- oatmeal
- long grain white rice
- yogurt
- most fruits

Moderate- and high-GI foods

Eat after sporting event:

- granola bar
- crispy rice
- corn flakes
- brown rice
- melon
- pita bread
- English muffin
- baked potato
- white bread
- sports drinks

Don't forget water!

An average person may lose as much as a quart of fluid during one hour of exercise. When you are not drinking enough fluids, your muscles quickly tire and you may develop leg cramps. Always remember to drink plenty of water before, during, and after exercise.

Training a Winning Mind

As a personal trainer, I help my clients develop a winning mind. This mindset is the ability to maintain focus, control emotions, and work effectively. It can make the difference between winning and losing. Often the key to achieving peak performance is managing your emotions.

The winning qualities of champions

My most successful clients have the following mental qualities:

Desire—You want your goal so badly, you won't stop until you achieve it

Enthusiasm and passion—Passion and purpose equals motivation

Determination and persistence—Staying focused on the goal, even when losing

Concentration—The ability to focus on the task at hand

Confidence—The quiet assurance that you can, and will, win

Positive attitude—Positive desire and belief in oneself

Courage—Courage is not the absence of fear, but it's feeling the fear and doing it anyway

Self-awareness—Understanding the signals from your body and mental state, and allowing yourself time to rest, relax, and sleep

In the zone

With my clients, I emphasize that they must find their zone—a mental state of calmness and confidence where the athlete is totally in the here-and-now. There is total focus, and actions and decisions seem effortless and easy.

The secret to becoming good at something quickly is modeling. Modeling is finding out how somebody does something, and then adopting and adapting their approach to suit your own purposes.

I show my clients how to identify and study champions. Then I point out the techniques that they can apply in their own sports.

Athletes can save themselves years of practice by studying how someone else does something and then borrowing the approach.

Personal Training and Coaching Tips

To be an effective personal trainer, you must be a good leader. Leaders are people who can motivate, guide, and direct others to give their best. Leaders are made through discipline, training, experience, and the desire to continually improve. Here are some tips for becomming a good leader.

Learn to be strong but not rude

It is important to stay relaxed and friendly when leading others. Being a trainer can be stressful, but good trainers know how to stay relaxed and get their message across.

Understand your client or team members

Understand what really motivates them. Care enough to see whether there's anything holding them back or preventing them from achieving their best. Always remember, praise is one of the greatest motivators of all.

Set goals

Achieving goals is a great motivator. It's also helpful to break a big dream into small achievable steps.

Never be negative

Focus on successes rather than failures. Build on strengths rather than weaknesses.

Keep a sense of humor

Always remember that sports are meant to be fun!

PUN FUN The personal trainer quit his job because it wasn't working out.

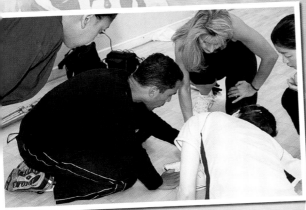

Lead by example

Use the right mental techniques so you can teach the importance of the mind in sport. Show clients how to stay positive, overcome defeat, and manage emotions. Use visualization techniques to teach skills and improve drills.

Shaun's Training Countdown Begins

Two days after the game, Shaun and I meet. We watch the game on video and look at areas where Shaun could have done better. We note the things he did that were great (like shoot the winning hoop). Shaun is still motivated by the win, and it shows in his eagerness to train. Shaun's goals this training session are to increase his speed and agility and to stay focused while practicing ball skills.

We begin our session with warm-up exercises. Warming up is a must, especially if you are coming back from an injury. While warming up, I get Shaun to focus and concentrate on his goals for this training session.

We concentrate on protecting the basketball. Shaun makes sure he has his knees bent and dribbles low. Shaun concentrates on being master of the ball. He can pass it high and soft or fast and low, and change the speed of a ball in a second. His first dribble can look weak and his second look strong.

We spend 30 minutes going over basic ball skills—handling, passing, and dribbling. To be the best basketball guard possible, Shaun must have these skills down so well they are second nature. This will help him find his zone like in the last game. Being good at the game's simplest skills makes the more difficult moves easier.

We do speed drills with the ball. I get Shaun to think about being quick with the ball, since basketball is a game of speed and agility.

Speed on the court is essential for success.

We practice game tactics and playing speed. These skills will help Shaun outperform others. We spend 10 minutes doing free-throw shooting. Shaun must make 12 shots in a row before the session is over. We end with more stretches. Shaun and I meet two more times before the championships. By the time the big game arrives, Shaun and his team are determined to win.

The big day arrives

The roar of the crowd is deafening. They start chanting Shaun's name. I wonder if he even notices. I've never seen Shaun play with such a burning desire to win. His focus and determination have motivated the rest of his team, keeping them in front by one point.

It's been a fast and tight game, and everyone's tired. But Shaun has remembered the tactics we practiced. The speed and the tone of the game change when he gains control. He still has energy. His team has noticed that if they get the ball to Shaun, they are virtually guaranteed to get it down to their end.

Shaun intercepts the ball and gains control. He dribbles it low and controls the game's speed. He toys with the defense as he waits for one of his team to get clear and take a shot. Suddenly he sees a break and tosses the ball high and long. His teammate explodes into a leap and tips the ball into the basket.

The crowd roars. The other team slumps in defeat. I notice two college scouts on the other side of the stadium pointing out and discussing Shaun. Shaun's team has won, and it looks as if Shaun is one step closer to being selected for the elite and competitive world of college basketball.

Being part of the journey of people achieving their dreams and tasting sports victory is one of the greatest rewards of being a personal trainer.

Coaches and scouts tour the country looking for talented athletes.

Practice being your own sports trainer

- Do your own fitness test.
- Set a goal to work toward.
- Find a training partner.
- Get out of your comfort zone—try something new.
- Learn about the human body and sports.
- Find a role model.
- Join a team or volunteer at a sports club.

Try something new!

Start a training diary

Date	Exercise	Duration	Ate/Drank	How I felt
10/12	Jog	30 minutes	Banana/ Water	Tired at start, but felt energized after the run. In good mood afterward.
10/14	Gym	60 minutes	Almonds/ Water	Feeling good to begin with, tired a little during the workout but felt great after.
10/17	Tennis	60 minutes	Sports Drink	Started really enthusiastically and managed to maintain this throughout game!
10/18	Hockey	60 minutes	Banana/Sports Drink	After tennis yesterday, felt drained but as the game progressed got into it. Tired later.
10/21	Jog	45 minutes	Granola Bar before run/Water	Felt really energized and happy after this well-paced lengthy run.

Steps to Become a Personal Trainer

You have two options for achieving your goal of becoming a personal trainer.

Option 1

Earning a college degree

Step One

Finish your secondary schooling, getting the best grades possible in all subjects. Certain subjects will be especially helpful for work as a personal trainer. Biology helps with understanding how the body works, and physical education is obviously very important for the job.

Step Two

Continue your education to earn a college degree. A degree in exercise physiology, physical education, sports science, applied science, or nursing will give you the skills you need. It will also give you options, if you decide in the future that you need a change, or are injured and forced to change careers.

Opportunities for personal trainers

Personal trainers can find work at many places:

- Personal trainer based at a club, league, or association
- Personal trainer working for a national sports organization
- Running your own training business
- Working at a gym
- With a degree, you can work as a physical education teacher

44

You can become a personal trainer without a college degree.

Step One

Complete an accredited course to become a personal trainer. These courses usually require that you are at least 18 years old and have a high school degree. Subjects studied include injury management, warm-ups, stretching, cool-downs, taping, nutrition, introduction to drugs in sports, and medical conditions.

Step Two

Once you complete the initial stage, it is possible to specialize even further in a field that suits your needs. Subjects include negligence and duty of care, wound management, sports psychology, principles of rehabilitation, drugs in sport, dental injuries, and concussion management.

Remember, when you do get a job, it will involve long hours. If you work for yourself, finding the time for vacation can be a challenge. You have to juggle your needs with those of your clients. However, having a love of sports and physical health will help spur you on in a sometimes difficult, but very rewarding, job.

Find Out More

In the Know

- Employment opportunites for personal trainers are expected to grow faster than average because the fitness industry is growing rapidly.
- Most personal training jobs are part-time positions. Trainers often increase their hours by working at more than one business or at clients' homes.
- Night and weekend hours are common.
- A recent report shows 7 percent of all fitness workers, including personal trainers, were self-employed.
- Average annual earnings in 2006 were $31,700. The lowest 10 percent earned less than $14,900 and the highest 10 percent earned more than $56,700.

Further Reading

Flender, Nicole. *Cool Careers Without College for People who Love Movement*. New York: Rosen Publishing Group, 2002.

Hofstetter, Adam B. *Cool Careers Without College for People who Love Sports*. New York: Rosen Publishing Group, 2007.

Mason, Paul. *Training for the Top*. Chicago: Raintree, 2006.

Reeves, Diane Lindsey. *Career Ideas for Kids Who Like Sports*. New York: Checkmark Books, 2007.

On the Web

For more information on this topic, use FactHound.

1. Go to *www.facthound.com*
2. Type in this book ID: 0756536197
3. Click on the *Fetch It* button.

Glossary

amateur—athlete who is not paid for playing a sport

baseline fitness—measure of a person's level of fitness before starting a training program

carbohydrates—sugars, starches, and fiber; a major source of energy for humans

circuit training—form of training that involves moving quickly between many different exercise machines

cool down—light exercise and stretching, which lessens muscle soreness; done after a workout or game

core strength—development of the abdominal and back muscles that surround the core area of the body

dehydration—loss of fluids from the body

insulin—chemical substance produced by the pancreas, which controls the amount of sugar in the blood; it moves sugar into the cells, where it can be used by the body for energy

ligament—band of tissue that connects or supports bones and joints

marathon—long-distance event based on an ancient Greek event; distance is just over 26 miles

metabolic rate—rate at which food is converted into energy

minerals—nutrients needed by the body in small amounts to help it function properly and stay strong

Pilates—strength-training movements involving coordinated breathing techniques; developed in Germany by Dr. Joseph Pilates during the 1920s

rehabilitation—returning an athlete to normal activities after injury

sprain—injury to a ligament caused by tearing or stretching

stability ball—large inflated rubber ball used for exercises and rehabilitation

starting blocks—blocks providing support for a runner's feet at the start of a race

warming up—gradual warming of the muscles through light exercise that lessens the likelihood of injuries while working out or playing a sport

Index

aerobic exercise, 26, 27, 28
anaerobic exercise, 26, 28
anatomy, 14, 15

biology, 14, 15
body types, 22, 23
bones, 18, 19, 27

carbohydrates, 30
chemistry, 14, 15
coaches, 6, 17

dieticians, 17

ectomorphs, 23
education, 12, 14, 15, 44, 45
endomorphs, 23
equipment, 23
exercise, 8, 26–28
exercise physiologists, 16
exercise physiology, 14

fats, 31
first aid. See injuries.
fitness tests, 24, 25, 43
food science, 14
foods. See nutrition.
friendliness, 36

glucose levels, 32
glycaemic index (GI), 32, 33
glycogen, 30
goals, 8, 9, 10, 29, 34, 37, 38, 43

heart, 24, 27
heart rate, 24, 25, 27
humor, 37

injuries, 5, 8, 9, 14, 18, 19
iron, 31

job description, 8–9
job opportunities, 44
joints, 9, 18, 29

kinesiology, 14

leadership, 36, 37

mesomorphs, 23
metabolic rate, 27
modeling, 35
motivation, 6, 9, 34–35, 36, 38, 41
muscles, 19, 20, 21, 22, 24, 27, 28, 29

nutrition, 30–32, 33

oxygen, 26, 31

physiology, 14
praise, 36
proteins, 30

recovery, 5, 8, 9, 16, 19

skeletal system, 18
skills, 8, 13, 37, 38, 40, 45
sports journalists, 17
sports managers, 16
sports officials, 17
sports physicians, 16
sports science, 9
stretching, 8, 11, 40, 44

therapy routines, 9
timetables, 10–11
training diaries, 43
training schedules, 6, 7, 18
training sessions, 7, 9, 38–40
triathlons, 12
twitch fibers, 20

warm-up exercises, 38, 44
water, 33
work environment, 9, 44

Look for More Books in This Series:

Art in Action: Have You Got What It Takes to Be an Animator?

Battling Blazes: Have You Got What It Takes to Be a Firefighter?

Cordially Invited: Have You Got What It Takes to Be an Event Planner?

Creating Cuisine: Have You Got What It Takes to Be a Chef?

Hard Hat Area: Have You Got What It Takes to Be a Contractor?

Pop the Hood: Have You Got What It Takes to Be an Auto Technician?

Sea Life Scientist: Have You Got What It Takes to Be a Marine Biologist?

Trendsetter: Have You Got What It Takes to Be a Fashion Designer?

Wild About Wildlife: Have You Got What It Takes to Be a Zookeeper?